Christmas Carols for RAGTIME PIANO

T0066227

CONTENTS

Cherry Lane Music Company
Director of Publications/Project Editor: Mark Philips
ISBN 978-1-60378-525-9

Visit our website at www.cherrylaneprint.com

Angels We Have Heard on High

Traditional French Carol

Moderately slow

Away in a Manger

Traditional

Deck the Halls

Traditional Welsh Carol

Moderately slow

9

The First Noël

17th Century English Carol

11

Go Tell It on the Mountain

African-American Spiritual

Moderately fast

13

Jingle Bells

Words and Music by
J. Pierpont

God Rest Ye Merry, Gentlemen

19th Century English Carol

Moderately slow

Hark! The Herald Angels Sing

Music by
Felix Mendelssohn-Bartholdy

Moderately slow

It Came upon the Midnight Clear

Music by
Richard S. Willis

Slowly

25

Joy to the World

Music by
George Frideric Handel

Moderately

D.S. al Fine

28

O Holy Night

Music by
Adolphe Adam

O Christmas Tree

Traditional German Carol

Moderately slow, relaxed

O Come, All Ye Faithful
(Adeste Fideles)

Music by
John Francis Wade

Moderately fast

O Little Town of Bethlehem

Music based on
Traditional English Melody

Moderately slow

We Three Kings of Orient Are

Words and Music by
John H. Hopkins, Jr.

Very slowly

40

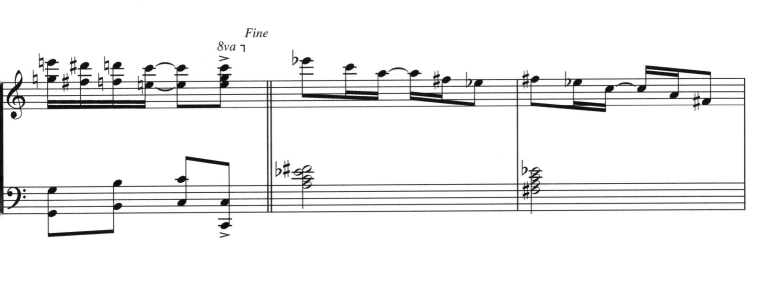

Silent Night

Music by
Franz X. Gruber

We Wish You a Merry Christmas

Traditional English Folksong

Moderately

What Child Is This?

16th Century English Melody

YOUR FAVORITE MUSIC
ARRANGED FOR PIANO SOLO

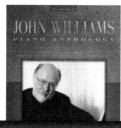

ARTIST, COMPOSER, TV & MOVIE SONGBOOKS

**Adele for Piano Solo –
3rd Edition**
00820186................................ $19.99

The Beatles Piano Solo
00294023................................ $17.99

**A Charlie Brown
Christmas**
00313176................................ $19.99

**Paul Cardall –
The Hymns Collection**
00295925................................ $24.99

Coldplay for Piano Solo
00307637................................ $17.99

**Selections from
Final Fantasy**
00148699................................ $19.99

**Alexis Ffrench – The
Sheet Music Collection**
00345258................................ $19.99

Game of Thrones
00199166................................ $19.99

Hamilton
00354612................................ $19.99

**Hillsong Worship
Favorites**
00303164................................ $14.99

How to Train Your Dragon
00138210................................ $22.99

Elton John Collection
00306040................................ $24.99

La La Land
00283691................................ $16.99

John Legend Collection
00233195................................ $17.99

Les Misérables
00290271................................ $22.99

Little Women
00338470................................ $19.99

Outlander: The Series
00254460................................ $19.99

**The Peanuts®
Illustrated Songbook**
00313178................................ $29.99

**Astor Piazzolla –
Piano Collection**
00285510................................ $19.99

**Pirates of the Caribbean –
Curse of the Black Pearl**
00313256................................ $22.99

Pride & Prejudice
00123854................................ $17.99

Queen
00289784................................ $19.99

John Williams Anthology
00194555................................ $24.99

George Winston Piano Solos
00306822................................ $22.99

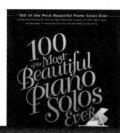

MIXED COLLECTIONS

**Beautiful Piano
Instrumentals**
00149926................................ $19.99

**Best Jazz
Piano Solos Ever**
00312079................................ $27.99

**Big Book of
Classical Music**
00310508................................ $24.99

Big Book of Ragtime Piano
00311749................................ $22.99

Christmas Medleys
00350572................................ $16.99

Disney Medleys
00242588................................ $19.99

Disney Piano Solos
00313128................................ $17.99

Favorite Pop Piano Solos
00312523................................ $17.99

Great Piano Solos
00311273................................ $19.99

**The Greatest Video
Game Music**
00201767................................ $19.99

Most Relaxing Songs
00233879................................ $19.99

**Movie Themes
Budget Book**
00289137................................ $14.99

**100 of the Most Beautiful
Piano Solos Ever**
00102787................................ $29.99

100 Movie Songs
00102804................................ $32.99

Peaceful Piano Solos
00286009................................ $19.99

**Piano Solos for
All Occasions**
00310964................................ $24.99

Sunday Solos for Piano
00311272................................ $17.99

Top Hits for Piano Solo
00294635................................ $16.99

HAL•LEONARD®
View songlists online and order from your
favorite music retailer at
halleonard.com

*Prices, content, and availability subject
to change without notice.*

Disney characters and artwork TM & © 2021 Disney